364.1524 M48w
Melanson, Philip H.
Who killed Martin Luther
 King?

Luther King?

Philip Melanson

edited by
Sandy Niemann

OdONiAN PRESS
BERKElEY, CAliFORNiA

Additional copies of this book and others in the Real Story series are available for $5 + $2 shipping per *order* (not per book) from Odonian Press, Box 7776, Berkeley CA 94707. To order by credit card, or for information on quantity discounts, please call us at 800 REAL STORY, or 510 524 4000. Distribution to book stores and book wholesalers is through Publishers Group West, Box 8843, Emeryville CA 94662, 510 658 3453 (toll-free: 800 788 3123).

Final editing and inside design: Arthur Naiman
Page layout and production coordination: Karen Faria
Index: Steve Rath   Series editor: Arthur Naiman
Series coordinator: Susan McCallister
Printing: Michelle Selby, Jim Puzey / Consolidated Printers, Berkeley, California

Odonian Press gets its name from Ursula Le Guin's wonderful novel *The Dispossessed* (though we have no connection with Ms. Le Guin or any of her publishers). The last story in her collection *The Wind's Twelve Quarters* also features the Odonians.

Odonian Press donates at least 10% (last year it was 36%) of its aftertax income to organizations working for social justice.

Melanson, Philip H.
   Who killed Martin Luther King? / Philip Melanson
        p. cm.
   Includes bibliographical references and index.
   ISBN 1-878825-11-9 : $5.00
   1. King, Martin Luther, Jr., 1929–1968—Assassination I. Title.
E185.97.K5M394 1993
364.1'524'097309046—dc20   93–19961
                                                    CIP

Copyright © 1993 by Philip Melanson. All rights reserved, including the right to reproduce or copy this book, or any portions of it, in any form whatever (except for brief excerpts in reviews).
Printed in the United States of America   First printing, February 1993

Allen County Public Library
900 Webster Street
PO Box 2270
Fort Wayne, IN 46801-2270

Contents

Chapter One

Murder in Memphis

In March 1967, Martin Luther King, Jr. made a decision that may have cost him his life. He and his Southern Christian Leadership Conference (SCLC) denounced the war in Vietnam as "morally and politically unjust" and promised to do "everything in our power" to stop it.

In April, King stepped up his attack. At a speech at the Riverside church in New York City, he called the US "the greatest purveyor of violence in the world today" and compared American practices in Vietnam to Nazi practices in WWII. He challenged all young men eligible for the draft to declare themselves conscientious objectors.

Before this, King had kept his civil rights work separate from the peace movement, partly on the advice of other black leaders who felt racial justice should be his first goal. But he increasingly saw that "the giant triplets of racism, materialism and militarism" couldn't be separated. The war was siphoning off money desperately needed for the poor and racially oppressed at home.

So King planned "civil disobedience on a massive scale" in order "to cripple the operations of an oppressive society." There would be sit-ins of the unemployed at factory entrances across the country, "a 'hungry people's sit-in' at the Department of Labor" and a Poor People's March on Washington, where thousands of demonstrators of all races would pitch their tents in the nation's capitol and stay until they'd been heard. There were even rumors (though King denied them) that he might run in the 1968 presidential election on an antiwar, third-party ticket with Dr. Benjamin Spock.

King's actions brought sharp criticism from all sides, black and white alike. *Life* magazine called the Riverside speech "demagogic slander that sounded like a script for Radio Hanoi." It charged King with "introduc[ing] matters that have nothing to do with the legitimate battle for equal rights here in America."

Even the more moderate National Association for the Advancement of Colored People (NAACP) agreed: "To attempt to merge the civil rights movement with the peace movement," they said, "will serve the cause neither of civil rights nor of peace."

From the government there wasn't just hostility—there was fear. King had already demonstrated the ability to instigate massive unrest, and his rumored presidential candidacy would appeal to those appalled by the war.

For years the FBI had wiretapped King's home and office, intercepted phone conversations and planted paid informants within the SCLC; now it stepped up its surveillance. President Lyndon Johnson is said to have admitted privately, "That goddamn nigger preacher may drive me out of the White House."

Tensions were high and King's list of enemies was long when, the following spring, he came to Memphis to support a strike by (mostly black) sanitation workers who were demanding job safety, better wages and an end to racial discrimination on the job.

The murder

King visited Memphis twice in March 1968. On the 18th, he addressed a crowd of 17,000 supporters of the strike. He promised then that he'd return on March 28 to lead a citywide demonstration of sympathy for the workers.

The March 28 event erupted in violence. As demonstrators marched through the city, rampaging black youths broke store windows and looted. King tried to curtail the escalating violence by requesting that the demonstration be cut short. But by the time it was over, police had moved on the crowd, wielding mace, nightsticks and guns. One black youth was shot and killed, and 60 persons were injured. Nevertheless, King promised to return on April 3 to plan another demonstration; this time, he hoped, Memphis would see the power of his nonviolent approach.

King spent the last day of his life, April 4, 1968, closeted inside the Lorraine Motel on Mulberry Street, in one of Memphis' seedier neighborhoods. After a long day conferring with aides about the upcoming event, he was looking forward to a prime rib and soul food dinner at Rev. Samuel B. Kyles' home that evening.

Just before 6 pm, King and Kyles stepped out onto the second-floor balcony overlooking the motel's courtyard. King exchanged greetings with several persons who stood below, waiting to join him for dinner. Kyles headed downstairs to get his car. King stood alone on the balcony.

At 6:01 a single shot from a high-powered rifle cracked through the evening air. The bullet tore into the right side of King's face, tossing him violently backward.

Rev. Ralph Abernathy, who was inside splashing on a final dollop of after-shave lotion, heard the sound—like a "firecracker." He rushed to the door. All he could see were King's feet: the impact had sent him reeling diagonally backward. Rushing to King's side, he cried out to those below, "Oh my God, Martin's been shot." Then he tried to comfort his dying friend: "This is Ralph, this is Ralph, don't be afraid."

But King lay unconscious in an ever-widening pool of blood. By the time Andrew Young rushed up from the parking lot and checked for a pulse, he knew it was all over. Within five minutes an ambulance was speeding the victim to St. Joseph's hospital. At 7:05 pm, 39-year-old Martin Luther King, Jr. was pronounced dead.

Finding an assassin

When the country learned of King's death, riots broke out in more than 100 American cities, and thirty-seven people were killed. For the first time in our history, the White House situation room (the windowless cavern under the West Wing where the president and his closest advisors gathered to deal with crises in Vietnam, the Middle East and eastern Europe) was used to monitor a domestic crisis.

Law-enforcement personnel launched the largest manhunt ever—the search for the alleged assassin, Eric S. Galt (the name on the registration of the abandoned car which was thought to be the getaway vehicle). On April 5, US Attorney General Ramsey Clark called a press conference and assured the country that, "We are getting close [to an arrest]." He also stated that the case involved only one man and that there was no evidence of a conspiracy.

Clark's optimism proved unfounded. It wasn't until April 19 that investigators identified fingerprints on the gun thought to be the murder weapon. They knew then for the first time that the man they sought was James Earl Ray, not Eric S. Galt. Even so, Ray eluded capture until June 8, when he was caught in London trying to board a plane for Brussels.

Ray spent the next nine months preparing to go to trial. Then, unexpectedly, on March 10, 1969, he pleaded guilty and was sentenced to 99 years in prison.

Ray would later claim that he was coerced into the plea. He said his lawyer, Percy Foreman, threatened that he'd implicate Ray's brother Jerry in the King controversy, and that he'd send government authorities after Ray's

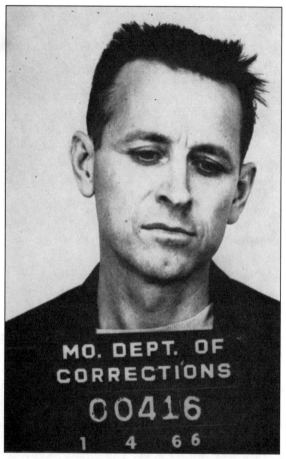

1966 prison mug shot of James Earl Ray

father and have him put back in the jail cell
from which he'd escaped more than 40 years
earlier. Ray claims that he was debilitated by
eight months in a sealed cell where lights

3 1833 02227 2998

glared 24 hours a day, cameras monitored his movements and two guards watched him constantly, so he finally succumbed to the threats.

The evidence against Ray

If the case against James Earl Ray were summarized by a prosecuting attorney, the evidence would read as follows:

Ray arrived in Memphis the day before the crime and checked into the New Rebel Motel using the alias Eric S. Galt. The next day he rented a room at Bessie Brewer's boarding house across from the Lorraine Motel, using the alias John Willard (see the next page for a map of the area).

Ray rejected a room that had no view of King's motel in favor of one that did. The furniture in the room was then moved around: a dresser was moved away from the window and a chair drawn up to the window, probably to surveil King. Ray also purchased a pair of binoculars after renting the room; the straps were found in the room.

One witness inside the rooming house, William Anschutz, claimed that in the hours just before the shooting, he had tried to use the second floor bathroom on two occasions, but found it occupied. Another tenant, Charles Stephens, told Anschutz that the new boarder (Ray/Willard) was using the bathroom. After hearing the shot, both Stephens and Anschutz ran into the hallway and saw a man running from the bathroom carrying a bundle.

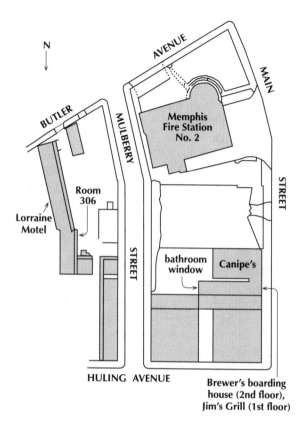

The scene of the crime

Minutes later, a bundle was dropped in the doorway of Canipe's Amusement Company, next door to the boarding house. Guy Canipe, the owner, and two customers, Bernell Finley and Julius Graham, heard the thud of the bundle as it dropped and glimpsed a man pass by. Canipe and Finley claimed that the man wore a dark suit and looked clean and neat. According to Bessie Brewer, Ray was wearing a dark brown suit and looked clean and neat compared with the local population.

Finley and Graham told authorities that after the thud, a white Mustang pulled away from the curb near Canipe's. Canipe also saw a car pull away but couldn't identify what kind it was. Memphis Police Officer Vernon Dollahite told the FBI that when he arrived at Canipe's minutes after the shooting, there was an empty parking space just north of the doorway and skid marks in the street, apparently made by an escaping vehicle. Ray admits to driving a "very pale yellow" Mustang that day.

In the bundle found in Canipe's doorway, police discovered a 30.06 Remington Gamesmaster rifle, binoculars, ammunition and a portable radio. Ray's prints were found on several items contained in the bundle. The serial number of the rifle matched the number of the one purchased by Ray in Birmingham, Alabama. The radio had an identification number which was partially scratched off, but the FBI was able to decipher it: it was Ray's inmate number at Missouri State Penitentiary. (Ray had escaped from the Penitentiary in April 1967 and had been on the run ever since.)

Ray's defense

Ray never defended himself in a trial, but in 1992 he published what he called "the true story" of his role in King's murder. Ray claimed to be in Memphis on a gunrunning deal with his on-again, off-again employer for the past nine months—a man named Raoul. They'd met in Montreal in July 1967 when Ray, recently escaped from prison, wanted fake travel papers to leave the country. Raoul promised them in exchange for smuggling and gunrunning.

In August, at Raoul's request, Ray bought a car—a 1966 pale yellow Ford Mustang—and the following March a "large bore deer rifle and scope," to show to prospective gunrunning clients. Raoul had Ray return the rifle for an even more powerful model and then instructed Ray to meet him in Memphis, with the rifle, on April 3.

On April 3 Ray checked into the New Rebel Motel as planned. On April 4, Ray met Raoul at 3 pm at Jim's Grill, a restaurant on the first floor of the building which housed Brewer's boarders on the second floor. Ray parked his car in front of Jim's, noting that the car ahead of his was the same color as his own. Once inside, Raoul suggested Ray rent an upstairs room at Brewer's, to meet with the gun runners. Ray did that; Raoul then sent him out to find some infrared binoculars the clients wanted.

Ray brought the binoculars back to Bessie's about 4 pm. For the next hour he was out getting a hamburger and going for a walk. When he returned about five, Raoul was still in the room; he asked Ray to stay out a while longer so he could meet the prospective clients alone. Not knowing quite what to do with himself, Ray sat outside in the car for a while, then decided to drive to a gas station to fix the spare tire (earlier that day, he'd noticed it was flat).

Driving back to Brewer's shortly after six, Ray found the area filled with policemen. One was directing traffic away from South Main Street, forcing Ray to redirect his route away from the boarding house. As an escaped fugitive, Ray decided to head out of town until things cooled down.

While driving he heard on the radio that King had been shot, and that police were looking for a white man in a white Mustang. All too aware that he closely matched that description, he headed for the state line and then for Atlanta, where he'd left some belongings from an earlier meeting with Raoul.

By the next morning, he'd wiped the interior and exterior of the car clean of fingerprints and abandoned it in an Atlanta parking lot. He caught a bus for Detroit that afternoon, then a train to Toronto—again hoping he might find a way to leave North America for good. This time he was more successful. After researching birth notices in the Toronto Evening Telegram for the year 1932, he picked the name Ramon George Sneyd and applied for a passport. On May 2 it arrived; on May 6 Ray was on his way to London.

In London, Ray tried to make contacts to help him reach his final goal—an English-speaking country in Africa. The cheapest way to get there, he reasoned, was to sign up with a military unit headed for the war in Nigeria. But as he was boarding a plane to Brussels to pursue military contacts there, he was apprehended by Scotland Yard investigators. By July 19, Ray was back in the US—in Shelby County Jail in downtown Memphis.

Reinvestigating the case

From the beginning, many believed that even though Ray had pleaded guilty, the full truth hadn't been revealed in the King case. But it wasn't until the mid 1970s, when the Senate Select Committee on Intelligence learned about the FBI's vendetta against King and the clandestine activities of US intelligence agencies generally, that there was sufficient support in Congress to reopen the case.

In 1977 Congress appointed the House Select Committee on Assassinations (HSCA) to review both the John F. Kennedy and King assassinations. The HSCA spent 2½ years and $6,000,000 investigating. In the King case, they determined that:

- Ray was the assassin
- he probably didn't act alone, but was encouraged by a racist, right-wing conspiracy
- "no federal, state, or local agency was involved in the assassination"

This book will examine the plausibility of each of these claims.

Chapter 2

Was Ray the assassin?

Is there sufficient evidence to convict Ray? The HSCA's story sounds persuasive, but a closer look at the effort to determine the sniper's location, and the fingerprint, ballistics and lie-detector evidence, shows it to be largely circumstantial and seriously flawed.

The sniper's location

Although it's often possible to determine the precise location of a sniper by plotting the trajectory path of the bullet, that's not possible in the King case. We'd need to know either King's exact position as he bent over the Lorraine Motel balcony railing or the path of the bullet as it moved through his body—and we don't know either. There aren't any photographs of King during the assassination (as there were, for example, of John Kennedy) and the bullet's path wasn't probed in the autopsy.

We only know that the bullet entered King's body from the right and at a slightly downward angle. That means the shot could have been fired from either the bathroom of the boarding house or by someone standing in the bushes below the bathroom window. (The boarding house yard was elevated above a concrete wall, so a shot fired by a man standing in the yard would have hit King's body at a downward angle.)

Still, the HSCA asserted that the assassin fired from the bathroom. To make this claim, they relied on two pieces of evidence: Ray's behavior when renting the room at Brewer's boarding house and, to a much greater extent, the earwitness testimony of other boarders.

Renting the room

The HSCA's final report describes Ray's renting of the room as if it's part of his premeditated assassination plan. But was it?

If Ray was planning to shoot King from the boarding house, he certainly made no attempt to be inconspicuous. Bessie Brewer told the FBI that her initial impression of Ray, who was wearing a dark suit and tie, was that he did not "fit in" with the other tenants and looked as though he could have obtained lodging in "nicer surroundings." Virtually everyone who saw the "new tenant" clearly remembered the neatly dressed man in the dark suit.

It's true that Ray did reject the first room offered to him. But there was a good reason—it wasn't a private room. Ray was a fugitive and in Memphis on illegal business; both made privacy essential. When Ray was shown another, private room (5-B) in the north wing, he took it without hesitation, never checking the view from the window.

It's also true that, as the HSCA points out, the room Ray ultimately selected was much nearer the bathroom than the one he rejected. But had Ray already decided to shoot from the bathroom? Mrs. Brewer recalled that after

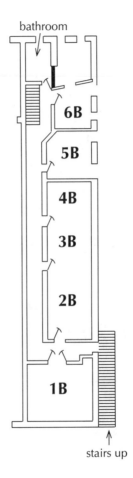

bathroom

6B

5B

4B

3B

2B

1B

stairs up

The second floor of Brewer's boarding house

saying he'd like the new room, Ray asked her where the bathroom was. If he knew the bathroom was to be his sniper's nest, he needn't have asked. If he was asking because he hoped to throw authorities off his trail later, it seems likely he'd have thought to dress less conspicuously as well.

If Ray did plan to assassinate King from the boarding house, his planning seems quite sketchy, to say the least. In order to see King's room from room 5-B, it was necessary to lean slightly out of the window, and risk being seen. And the bathroom could only be used for the shot if Ray positioned himself inside an old-fashioned bathtub with steeply sloping sides.

He'd also have to be in the bathroom at just the right time—when King was visible. Since this common bathroom served thirteen other people, many of whom were alcoholics, it was probably used quite frequently.

If Ray was surveilling from his room, then at the moment King appeared, he would have to gather up the bundle containing the radio, beer cans and cartridges, add the binoculars, and go up the hall to the bathroom, hoping it wasn't occupied. If Ray didn't take the bundle with him, then he'd have to go back to his room for it after the shooting, postponing his escape. And unless he brought the rifle box into the bathroom, he'd risk being seen with the gun.

The witnesses

The HSCA relied most heavily on the testimony of two boarders at Brewer's—Charles Stephens and, to a lesser extent, William Anschutz.

Stephens and his wife Grace shared room 6-B, which is between Ray's room and the bathroom. In 1968, the 46-year-old Stephens told the FBI that on several occasions during the afternoon, he'd heard the door to Ray's room open and someone go down the hall and into the bathroom. The person remained in the bathroom for "a considerable period of time." Yet during these visits Stephens heard the commode flush only once. On the last visit to the bathroom, Stephens estimated that it was occupied for 20–30 minutes.

Stephens claims to have been sitting in his kitchen repairing a radio when he heard a loud noise that he was sure was a gunshot. He was certain about the origin of the shot— it came from the bathroom next door, only a few feet away from where he was sitting.

When he heard the shot he ran to open his door (10–12 feet away) and saw a man running down the hall away from the bathroom. The man was carrying a package three to four feet long and six to eight inches thick, wrapped in what appeared to be newspaper. Stephens claimed he was in the hall when Anschutz came out of his apartment and said something to the fleeing man.

Stephens told the FBI that he only glimpsed the man from behind and didn't get a look at his face. He described the suspect as a "white male, 5' 10" or 5' 11", 165 pounds, slender, with a dark complexion, sandy or slightly dark hair, and wearing a dark suit." Stephens said the fugitive "closely resembled" the man who had earlier rented room 5-B. Stephens didn't see the man enter the hallway, so he couldn't say whether the man came directly from the bathroom or went from the bathroom to room 5-B and then ran down the hallway.

William Anschutz was in room 4-B, next to Ray's (on the opposite side from the Stephenses). He was watching TV when he heard a shot. He couldn't tell exactly where it came from, but he believed it was from either Ray's room or the bathroom.

Anschutz opened his door and saw a man running down the hall, hiding his face with his arm. The man was carrying something long; Anschutz thought it was wrapped in a blanket. As the man ran past, Anschutz claims to have said, "I thought I heard a shot." The man replied, "Yeah, it was a shot."

Anschutz thought the man had entered the hall from Ray's room but wasn't certain. He described the fugitive as six feet tall, slim and in his early thirties. The only thing Anschutz noticed about the man's clothing was that he didn't seem to be wearing a coat.

How reliable were these witnesses? Anschutz told the FBI that he wasn't drinking on the day of the assassination, and that he'd given up drinking for health reasons. This would make him one of the potentially more reliable witnesses at Brewer's. But Anschutz couldn't say whether the shot came from 5-B or the bathroom, and couldn't identify the fleeing suspect.

Only Stephens was sure that the shot definitely came from the bathroom, that the new tenant was spending a lot of time in the bathroom and that the fleeing figure "closely resembled" the new tenant. But an HSCA committee staff report, which was published in the committee's hearings and exhibits but not in the final report, describes Stephens as "well known on South Main Street for his excessive drinking habits." On the day of the assassination, Stephens had been in Jim's Grill "drinking—like always."

Although two police officers who questioned Stephens after the assassination noted that he was either "coherent" or "neither incoherent nor staggering," all acknowledged that he'd been drinking. And taxi driver James McGraw, who'd been summoned to pick up Stephens the afternoon of April 4, told the HSCA that he had seen Stephens lying on the bed in 6-B in a "drunken stupor."

There are other problems with Stephens' testimony. In 1968 he told the FBI in two separate interviews conducted three days apart that the man in the hallway "closely resembled" the man who had earlier checked into 5-B. Two months later, Stephens provided an affidavit used by US authorities in extraditing Ray from England. The closest Stephens would come to a positive identification of the fugitive was to say: "I think it was the same man I saw earlier with Mrs. Brewer looking at 5-B."

But in 1974 Stephens initiated a court proceeding to claim $185,000 in reward money for information leading to the arrest and conviction of King's killer. This time Stephens claimed that he had positively identified Ray as the fleeing suspect, from a photo provided by police after Ray's arrest. Other details of Stephen's story also changed.

In 1968 Stephens claimed Anschutz had tried to get into the bathroom earlier in the afternoon, but never mentioned trying to get into the bathroom himself. In 1974 Stephens claimed that he had tried to get in the bathroom several times and that immediately after the shot, "I went to the bathroom, opened the door, glanced in and then down the hall. This guy was just turning the corner down the hall."

There were, furthermore, three witnesses who saw or heard something indicating that the shot might have been fired from the bushes outside. Stephens' wife, Grace, was in bed ill in room 6-B. She told the FBI that she'd heard a noise like a firecracker that seemed to come from the yard behind the building.

She also claimed to have heard soft footsteps coming out of the bathroom and proceeding rapidly down the hallway. According to the HSCA report, Mrs. Stephens later claimed to have seen the fleeing fugitive but said that it was not Ray.

Harold Carter, another boarder, reportedly saw a man with a rifle running from the bushes. And Solomon Jones, King's chauffeur, who was in the Lorraine Motel parking lot, told the FBI that immediately after the shooting he glimpsed the back of a man in the shrubbed area behind the boarding house.

Given this contradictory and questionable testimony, it's a wonder that the HSCA could determine who to believe and who not to believe. But they did. The committee tried to discredit those witnesses whose testimony didn't support a shot from the bathroom.

They repeatedly stressed the inconsistencies in Grace Stephens' story, and then concluded that because she may have been drinking on April 4 and was committed to a mental hospital shortly after the assassination, her observation of someone other than Ray leaving the boarding house was "not worthy of belief." Carter's testimony was discounted because in 1968 Bessie Brewer had told the FBI he "drank considerably."

The committee also concluded that since Jones had been pushed to the ground by others in the Lorraine parking lot seconds after the shooting, and since by the time he got up police officers had "almost" arrived at the Lorraine, the man seen by Jones "may have been a law enforcement officer responding to the shot."

That view was reinforced by a Memphis police officer's report that he rushed into the backyard after the shot and had observed only two footprints near the cellar door, even though it had rained the day before. (Plaster casts were made of the footprints, but the results of this effort, if any, are unknown.)

But the HSCA didn't subject Charles Stephens' testimony to the same scrutiny. Although the committee acknowledged that his sobriety had been "called into question by a number of sources," they still relied on Stephens to link Ray to the bathroom and to establish that the shot was fired from the bathroom.

There was also no mention of the inconsistencies in his story, even though his pursuit of financial reward and his shifting accounts made him the kind of prosecution witness whose testimony would be severely discredited, if not torn to shreds, by any competent defense lawyer. Instead, Stephens' notions about what happened at the crime scene became a pillar of the committee's reconstruction.

Fingerprints

In 1968 the FBI photographed two fingerprints and one palm print on the alleged murder rifle. A decade later, the HSCA hired three fingerprint experts to see if these prints were in fact Ray's.

The first expert, Victor J. Scalice, positively identified all three prints on the rifle as Ray's prints, but couldn't positively identify a photograph of the print on the telescopic sight— it was too poor in quality. He also found Ray's prints on several items in the bundle: the binoculars, the newspaper and a Schlitz beer can.

When Scalice was called away by other commitments, two experts from the Washington

D.C. Metropolitan Police Department took over. Their findings differed markedly from Scalice's—they found positive identifications of Ray's prints on the telescopic sight of the rifle and on a bottle of aftershave lotion (which was also in the bundle), but couldn't positively identify any of the same prints Scalice did, including the three prints on the rifle that Scalice had identified as Ray's.

The HSCA chose to ignore the conflicting findings, and instead presented Scalice's findings as definitive. The final report states: "No prints, either identifiable or unidentifiable, other than Ray's, were found on the rifle."

The HSCA also made little of the fact that Ray's fingerprints didn't show up in places we'd expect them to. A spent cartridge—the one that allegedly held the bullet that killed King—was found in the rifle. Although the cartridge was hand-loaded into the rifle (according to the HSCA's ballistics experts) and its surface would retain fingerprints rather well, there were no prints at all on the cartridge case.

Nor were Ray's prints found on any of the nine bullets in the bundle. This is especially odd since the bullets were of two different types, and four had been placed in the box by someone other than the manufacturer. And the cardboard box in which the rifle was found yielded only one print—that of Donald Wood, the clerk at the gun shop where Ray originally purchased the rifle. Did Ray carefully avoid putting his prints on the bullets, the rifle box and on the cartridge case while loading it into the rifle, yet fail to wipe his prints from the scope and other items in the bundle?

Ray's prints weren't found in the boarding house either. Three of the ten prints Memphis police lifted from room 5-B and the bathroom were clear enough to permit identification. One, from the dresser in Ray's room, belonged to a Memphis policeman (even though the dresser had been moved away from the window, allegedly by Ray, as part of his attempts to monitor King). The second print, from the fireplace in Ray's room, has never been identified. The third, from the windowsill of the bathroom, belonged to an FBI agent.

Ballistics

The HSCA final report acknowledged that it couldn't say with certainty that the fatal shot was fired from the rifle Ray had purchased. But it concluded "that it was possible" for that to be the case.

When a bullet is fired from a rifle, it's marked in two ways—first, when the rifle firing pin hits the bullet cartridge and next when the bullet itself passes through the barrel. Since each rifle makes different markings, it's usually possible to determine whether a spent cartridge and bullet were fired from a particular rifle.

In the King case, the spent cartridge case found in Ray's rifle did bear the distinct markings of the firing pin of that rifle. So we know that the cartridge launched a bullet from that rifle at some indeterminate time. But we don't know if it launched the fatal bullet, since there's no way to link a bullet to a particular spent cartridge.

We also know that a fragment of the bullet removed from King's body manifested the class characteristics of a 30.06 caliber Remington Peters bullet—the same type of bullet used by the rifle found at the crime scene. But this fragment couldn't be positively identified as having been fired by Ray's rifle; that's because Ray's rifle, when tested, made different markings on every bullet shot from it.

So, while it's possible that the bullet that killed King was fired from Ray's rifle, there's no evidence to prove that it was. The HSCA report downplayed this fact.

The HSCA also neglected to pursue other ballistics questions or tests that could have shed light on the case. First, the bundle dropped at the crime scene contained an odd mix of ammunition. There were nine bullets of two different types—five were 30.06 caliber Springfield commercial-type ammunition, the same type as the fatal bullet; the others were military-type ammunition. The committee's firearms panel determined that the military-type bullets bore markings indicating that they previously "may have been loaded into disintegrating-type machine gun link belts or an eight-round clip for the MI Gerand rifle."

These aspects weren't probed; the committee didn't determine who bought the ammunition, where it was purchased and why two types of bullets were in one box.

Second, a neutron activation test could have helped link the fatal bullet to the other bullets in the bundle. In it, samples of bullets are bombarded with neutrons; it's then possible to compare the number and proportion of trace elements (copper, silver, sodium, etc.) that make up each bullet or fragment. The greater the similarity of composition, the more likely it is that bullets or fragments were manufactured in the same batch.

In 1968 the FBI performed a neutron activation test on the five commercial bullets found in the bundle, the spent cartridge found in the rifle and the fragments of the fatal bullet. They found that the bullets were made by the same manufacturer but that their elemental composition varied so much that they couldn't be used as a "standard" against which to compare the fatal bullet.

(The specific results of the FBI test remained classified, so we don't know the degree to which the bullets varied from one another. It's also not clear how the FBI knew the bullets came from the same manufacturer, since their composition varied so much.)

The HSCA chose not to redo this test, since the earlier one had been inconclusive. But a comparison of the five commercial bullets with the fatal bullet might well have yielded important data. Even if the five bullets weren't similar, fragments of the fatal bullet could have been compared to each of the five bullets, and the empty cartridge in the rifle could be compared to the other cartridge cases. If the empty cartridge or fatal bullet contained a trace element not found in any of the five bullets or cartridges—or if the same elements were present but in vastly smaller or larger quantities—it would tend to indicate that the fatal bullet or the empty cartridge didn't come from the same batch(es) of ammunition as the five bullets found in the box.

Third, the HSCA made little of the fact that the assassin loaded only one bullet into the rifle. As purchased, the rifle had a five-shot capacity—an ammunition clip held four shots and one additional bullet could be loaded into the chamber. No clip was ever found. But without it, the assassin's only possibility for a second shot was to handload the weapon (a time-consuming and therefore risky method).

If Ray was so inept as to lose the clip or so incompetent that he couldn't master its use, one can't help but wonder how he mustered the technical savvy and confidence to pull off the assassination. It's also difficult to imagine how Ray who, so far as we know, had never before shot at a human being and was not a skilled marksman, would have the confidence to assume that he needed only one shot.

Lie detector tests

When the HSCA's polygraph experts reviewed the results of two lie detector tests Ray had taken voluntarily in 1977, they found the tests seriously flawed. Some of the questions were poorly designed, the establishment of baseline response (patterns against which to measure the truth or falsity of the crucial questions) was inadequate and, in one test, "outside noises" and frequent interruptions by Ray's attorney created a poor environment. It's also possible that Ray's responses were affected by fatigue—the tests were administered almost back to back, in the early morning.

In addition, the HSCA panel noted "an apparent attempt by Ray to create artificial reactions to control questions." It appeared that "Ray had studied polygraph technique and attempted to produce lie-type reactions to the control questions," ostensibly to hide his real lies. (To do this, the subject depresses his arm in the "cardio cuff," producing an upward surge of blood pressure—the kind of surge typically associated with untruthful responses.)

And yet, even with all these questions about the test results, the panel asserted that some of the results were valid. The committee claimed that Ray was lying when he answered two questions negatively: "Do you know who shot Dr. Martin Luther King, Jr.?" and "Did you shoot Dr. Martin Luther King, Jr.?"

So where does the HSCA's case against Ray stand? Given the tenuousness of the evidence, the HSCA's firm assertion that James Earl Ray was the assassin can in no way be proven. His precise role in the crime, if any, must be determined in a future investigation.

Chapter 3

Evidence of a conspiracy

The HSCA's second most important finding was that while Ray had committed the crime alone, he was probably encouraged by a racist, right-wing element based in St. Louis—thus there was a conspiracy behind the murder. It's surprising that the committee was willing to adopt this theory as their final conclusion, since the evidence for it was so inconclusive.

The St. Louis conspiracy theory

The HSCA's interest in the St. Louis group was stimulated in large part by a 1974 FBI report in which Russell Byers, a St. Louis underworld figure, told an FBI informant that he had been offered money to assassinate King. When the HSCA investigated, Byers offered the following story.

In late 1966 or early 1967, an alleged drug dealer named John Kaufman approached Byers and asked if he would like to make $50,000. That very evening, Byers claimed, he and Kaufman went to the St. Louis home of John Sutherland, a wealthy patent attorney and right-winger.

They found Sutherland in his study, decked out in a Confederate colonel's uniform and hat, amidst a cache of Civil War memorabilia. When he offered $50,000 to kill King, or to arrange to have him killed, Byers responded he'd think it over and left. To

Byers' knowledge, nothing further developed from the meeting.

The HSCA not only found Byers' story credible but concluded that Ray was responding to Sutherland's offer, since there were some possible links between the two men—Dr. Hugh Maxey, a friend of Kaufman's who was the prison doctor at Missouri State Penitentiary while Ray was serving time there, and John Paul Spika, Russell Byers' brother-in-law and a fellow inmate of Ray's, who worked as an orderly in the prison hospital under Dr. Maxey.

A third possible link was the Grape Vine Tavern in St. Louis, owned by Ray's sister Carol and managed by his brother John. This rough-and-tumble bar was a place where underworld types and petty criminals went to make contacts, as well as a hotbed of right-wing politics. The local headquarters for George Wallace's American Independent Party (which Sutherland generously supported) was across the street; Wallace supporters often dropped in for drinks. The HSCA concluded that since John Kaufman frequented the Grape Vine, James Earl Ray could have heard of Sutherland's offer there.

But there's no firm evidence that any of these links ever materialized. As the HSCA admitted:

Ultimately...the Committee's investigation of the St. Louis conspiracy proved frustrating....Direct evidence that would connect the conspiracy in St. Louis to [the] assassination was not obtained....Nevertheless, in light of the several alternative routes established by the evidence through which information of the offer could have reached James Earl Ray, the committee concluded that it was likely that he was aware of the existence of the St. Louis offer.

Not everyone on the committee was able to support such tenuous reasoning. Then-congressman Christopher Dodd (D-CT) dissented:

The evidence which the committee musters may suggest the outlines of a conspiracy, but, in my opinion, it falls short. After reviewing the evidence I am unable to say with any degree of certainty who conspired with James Earl Ray or under what plan they were acting.

However, there are numerous other pieces of evidence in this case that suggest a conspiracy, and the HSCA either ignored or dismissed them. When these aspects are examined, it becomes even more obvious that the HSCA reached their conclusion prematurely.

The bundle drop

The bundle dropped in front of Canipe's Amusement Company was one of the chief pieces of evidence used to implicate Ray. When the FBI and the HSCA investigated it, they speculated that Ray dropped the bundle in panic, probably as a result of seeing one of the police officers who had arrived about two minutes after the shooting. There was no reason, the HSCA thought, to conclude that the bundle drop was a plant designed by someone else to point the finger toward Ray.

But several questions about the bundle drop remain unanswered. According to the witnesses in Canipe's, the dark-clothed man they saw didn't run as a panicked assassin might, nor did he simply dump the bundle quickly on the sidewalk. Instead, he appears to have dropped the bundle deliberately. As he walked toward his car, he detoured briefly from his escape vehicle, "stepp[ing] to the left and dropp[ing] the bundle in the recess [of Canipe's doorway]." Further, while Graham and Finley's descriptions could fit Ray, Canipe described a "chunky," dark-skinned (although Caucasian) man, and that doesn't sound like Ray.

Two white Mustangs

Press reports covering the assassination and FBI interviews established that there were two white Mustangs present at the crime scene. (Ray described his car as "pale yellow," but all official reports and witnesses describe his car and/or the second Mustang as "white.") One was parked almost directly in front of Jim's Grill (next door to the boarding house) and the other was several car lengths south, near the doorway to Canipe's (see the map on page 12).

Four men remembered seeing an empty Mustang in front of Jim's Grill. From their combined testimony, it seems that the car was there from around 3:55 pm to between 5:15 and 5:30 pm. The second Mustang, parked closer to Canipe's, was spotted between 4:30 or 4:45 and sometime after 5:00 by three employees of Seabrook Wallpaper Company as they waited for their rides home. These employees also noticed a white, dark-haired male sitting behind the wheel; by 5:20 (perhaps earlier) one of them noticed that there was no longer anyone in the car.

One car apparently left the area before six— two men approaching the corner of Main and Vance between 5:15 and 5:30 remembered seeing a white Mustang pass directly in front of them, disappearing east on Vance. A second Mustang screeched away within minutes after the bundle was dropped.

From Ray's known and alleged movements on April 4, it's most likely that the car in front of Jim's Grill was his. He checked in at Brewer's at about 3:30; according to the clerk at York Arms Company, he bought binoculars "about 4:00." Since the clerk's estimate is somewhat vague and York Arms is only about a mile and a half from the Grill, it's very possible that Ray was back shortly after four, close to the time the Mustang was spotted in front of Jim's Grill.

It's less likely that the second Mustang, parked near Canipe's, belonged to Ray. First, the car wasn't spotted until 4:30 or 4:45. Second, if Ray was the assassin, why would he arrive and park, then spend the next 30–45 minutes away from the boarding house rather than setting up the kill?

The presence of the two Mustangs is important for several reasons. First, simply the fact that two cars of the same make and color were both in the immediate crime scene area is suspicious. Second, since the car in front of Jim's Grill left the area sometime between 5 and 5:30, there's possible corroboration for Ray's story that he left the area to fix the spare tire between 5 and 6.

Two dark suits

According to Bessie Brewer, Ray stood out from others in the neighborhood because he dressed in a suit. But on April 4 and 5, there was a second man in the neighborhood wearing a dark suit. The HSCA chose not to investigate that fact.

The morning after the assassination, the owner of Jim's Grill, Lloyd Jowers, called the police about a mysterious stranger who was eating breakfast and "acting strange"—he seemed "very calm" while everyone else appeared agitated over the shooting. Jowers had also noticed this same man at about 4 pm the day before, when he'd ordered a meal at the Grill. Jowers described him as a "white male, 5' 8" to 5' 9", heavy (about 160 pounds), with a ruddy complexion and sandy hair, and wearing a dark suit."

The dark-suited man (whom I'll call Ted Andrews to protect his identity) was stopped by the police that morning and taken to headquarters for questioning. He claimed to have left his home in Tennessee and hitchhiked all night to get to Memphis, catching a ride in a truck hauling pigs and arriving at 7:30 in the morning on April 4.

Between 9:30 and 10:00 am, he took a taxi to Helen Wynne's rooming house at 390½ Main Street, not far from Brewer's boarding house at 418–22½ Main. He claims that he had a meal at Jim's Grill around 2:00 and that just before 6:00, he walked from Mrs. Wynne's to the Ambassador Hotel, one block away, to make a phone call.

The FBI didn't fingerprint Andrews on the spot, but instead decided to obtain his prints from his Navy file. If they did so, the results remain unknown. The Bureau then cleared Andrews because "it appeared that he did not fit the available description of the unknown assailant and that information furnished by him as to his identity and activities in Memphis had been sufficiently verified to eliminate him as a suspect."

But this wasn't exactly the case. Although Andrews was shorter and weighed less than Ray, both had blue eyes and brown hair; both were conspicuous because they dressed in dark suits and were described as neat and clean. Even Andrews' wife later admitted that there was "a resemblance" between the two men.

There were also some oddities in Andrews' story. First, Mrs. Wynne said Andrews arrived at her home about 2 pm and went out to make phone calls at 5:30; the owner of Jim's Grill saw him eating about 4 pm. Both accounts differ from Andrews'. (When I interviewed Andrews in 1985 and again in 1989, he gave yet another story. When asked what he was doing when King was shot, he claimed, "I was having dinner in a restaurant.")

Second, Andrews claimed he'd come to Memphis to see if he could find someone who wanted a car driven to California where he had urgent business. But it wasn't clear why he needed to come to Memphis since two days earlier he'd been in Little Rock, Arkansas, which is several hundred miles closer to his California destination.

(In the later interviews, he claimed he'd come to Memphis to "sell some things." The central element of his earlier story—that he was trying to get to California—was absent.)

The Bureau itself fueled curiosity about Andrews by deleting sections of their documents on him. One deletion was 2½ lines long: "His presence near the scene around the time of the shooting [2½ lines deleted] indicated the desirability of his being questioned as a general suspect." The bottom of this same page indicates that this document is "to be destroyed."

Two other deletions relate to Andrews' military service—his selective service number is deleted, as well as an entire category of data comprising one-third of a page. These deletions are suspicious because they don't appear to be designed to protect his identity—other personal data remained in the file.

Raoul

The HSCA did investigate Ray's claim that he was in Memphis because of an alleged gun-running deal for Raoul. But they concluded Raoul didn't exist, both because Ray's physical description of Raoul varied from time to time and because there wasn't a single known witness who saw Ray and Raoul together during their 12–15 alleged meetings.

The committee decided that because six witnesses claimed Ray had at times referred to visiting, meeting or getting money from his "brother," "the tale of Raoul was fabricated to conceal contacts with one or both [of Ray's] brothers." The HSCA dismissed as "worthless" the brothers' explanation that "brother" was James' euphemism for Raoul.

The HSCA also dismissed evidence of the existence of a Raoul-like character who, although never seen with Ray, might corroborate some of Ray's story. In 1968, Andy Salwyn, then Montreal bureau chief for the Toronto Star, had searched the neighborhood near the Neptune Bar in Montreal where Ray had reportedly first met Raoul (in July 1967). He didn't find Raoul but did find evidence indicating that a Jules Ricco Kimble, a mysterious American known as "Rolland" or "Rollie," was in the right neighborhood at the right time.

Salwyn tracked down Rollie's girlfriend, Maryanne Levesque (I've changed her name to protect her identity) and learned that Rollie had a police-band radio in his car and was always asking her to translate police broadcasts, had guns in the trunk of his car, and had made a number of phone calls to the US from her apartment. She'd saved the bills, hoping to collect from him, and had turned them over to the Royal Canadian Mounted Police (RCMP).

The HSCA followed up by obtaining RCMP files, and interviewing Salwyn, Kimble and his wife, and New Orleans investigator Joseph Oster (who had investigated Kimble for the Louisiana Labor-Management Commission of Inquiry in 1967 and had traced Kimble's whereabouts for most of July to October of that year). They decided that since Oster had located Kimble in Montreal in September 1967, Oster's story conflicted with both Ray's story and Salwyn's data that placed Raoul-Kimble there in July. It concluded that there was therefore "no evidence to support a Ray-Kimble connection or to indicate Kimble was involved in any plot to kill Dr. King."

But the committee's investigation again proved to be superficial. Oster's findings didn't preclude the possibility that Kimble was in Montreal before September, for Oster had lost track of Kimble from July 18 until "sometime after July 21." Ray arrived in Montreal on July 18, at exactly the time Kimble couldn't be accounted for. The committee also passed over Oster's evidence that Kimble was in New Orleans in December 1967, when Ray claims to have met Raoul in a bar and received money from him.

The committee also downplayed some of the more provocative information in Oster's file. The HSCA report blandly mentions Kimble's "associations in 1967 with the Ku Klux Klan." According to Oster (whom I contacted independently), his file mentions that Kimble had meetings with Klan leaders in February and March 1967, and that he met with four Grand Dragons of the KKK on July 18, 1967, just before he disappeared for several days. Kimble's wife reported to Oster that she saw guns and explosives in the trunk of his car that same day.

Recently it's become clear that Kimble, who's now 45 and serving a double life sentence for racketeering and murder, should be an important focus for reinvestigating the case. When BBC documentary filmmakers Edginton and Sergeant interviewed Kimble in 1989, he admitted that he knew Ray, that he'd participated in the conspiracy to murder King, and that he'd told this to HSCA investigators.

(This last can't be verified, since the committee files are sealed till 2028. A CIA file on Kimble is footnoted in the HSCA's final report, but it's never been seen by anyone beyond CIA and the HSCA.)

Kimble also claimed to know the assassination scenario (which will be discussed in Chapter 4). He said his role was to pilot Ray from Atlanta to Montreal in July 1967 to meet with a CIA identities specialist. Edginton and Sergeant pursued this lead by contacting a retired CIA agent who had direct

knowledge of the agency's Montreal operations in the late 1960s. When Sergeant, not
revealing he had an interest in Kimble or the
King case, queried this ex-agent, he confirmed that the identities specialist had been
in Montreal in July 1967, and expressed surprise that that information had been found
out. But even more surprising for Edginton
and Sergeant was the fact that the specialist—Raoul Miora—had the same first name
as Ray's alleged employer.

Who, then, is Raoul? If he exists, is he
Kimble, or Raoul Miora? If Kimble's story
about Raoul Miora is true or partially true, it
may mean that Ray's "Raoul" is a composite
figure rather than just one operative. Some of
Kimble's actions are similar to those Ray
attributes to Raoul; Ray has never mentioned
the identities specialist, but he's also never
adequately accounted for how he obtained
his aliases (described in the next section).

Ray's aliases

During the nine-month period leading up to
the assassination, Ray used five different aliases. He first used the name Eric Starvo Galt in
Montreal in July 1967. He also established credentials for it—an Alabama driver's license,
and various letters and certificates—and used
it as his main alias for the next nine months.

In March 1968, he used the name Harvey
Lowmeyer to buy the rifle the HSCA says he
used to kill King. When he arrived in Memphis
the day before the assassination, he checked

into the New Rebel Motel as Galt. Then, the day of the assassination, he checked into Brewer's boarding house as John Willard. This was his only use of the Willard alias, for which he had no credentials or paper trail.

When he fled to Toronto after the assassination, Ray first used his old standby, the Galt alias. Then he took a room on Ossington Street under the name Paul E. Bridgeman, and later another room on Dundas Street under the name Ramon George Sneyd. Finally, Ray obtained a false Canadian passport in Sneyd's name and flew to London.

The fact that Ray used aliases was in itself nothing new—in his life of crime he'd frequently used them to hide his identity. But before the King assassination he'd always selected the names of people he knew—family members or people he knew in prison—because they were easy to remember.

But with the King case, four of his five aliases were the names of Canadian citizens living near Toronto. Ray wasn't familiar with any of these men and had never been to Toronto before the assassination. (The one exception was Harvey Lowmeyer; a man named Harvey Lohmeyer had worked in a prison kitchen with Ray's brother John.)

The HSCA described the Toronto aliases as "a matter of primary interest because of the almost unbelievable nature of the coincidences involved" and because of the "possible sinister implications" of Ray's ability to develop them. These coincidences included the following:

- In 1968, Ray was 40 years old, 5' 10", weighed approximately 170–175 pounds and had brown hair. Three of the men whose names he used as aliases—Galt, Bridgeman and Sneyd—very closely resembled Ray in height, weight and hair coloring. Willard was the least compatible of the four—he was two inches shorter and 20 pounds lighter. But, like Ray, both Willard and Galt had scars on their faces—Ray's and Galt's were above the right eye, Willard's below.

- All four men lived in Scarborough, a sixty-square-mile sprawling mix of suburban neighborhoods and industrial complexes on Toronto's eastern boundary. Galt, Sneyd and Bridgeman lived in a triangular cluster, approximately 1¾ miles from each other. Willard lived about three miles south of this triangle.

- Up until 1966, Galt abbreviated his middle name, St. Vincent, with the initials "St. V." He had a very distinctive way of signing the initials—he drew circles for the two periods, resulting in a unique, difficult-to-read scrawl that looked remarkably like Starvo. When Ray first used the Galt alias, he used the name Eric Starvo Galt. Then he switched to Eric. S. Galt—the same switch the real Galt made in 1966.

- Several years before the assassination, Galt had plastic surgery performed on the tip of his nose. Four months before the assassination, Ray had precisely the same surgery done. The HSCA, not knowing about Galt's surgery, reasoned that Ray was preparing for

*Top left: Paul Bridgeman. Top right: Eric S. Galt.
Bottom left: Ramon George Sneyd. Bottom right:
James Earl Ray.*

the crime by ridding himself of his sharply pointed nose. It made him look less distinctive and less like his old prison mug shots. But whether Ray knew it or not, the surgery also made him look more like Galt (and other Canadian aliases). Ray also adopted a hairstyle similar to Galt's and the others'.

How did Ray find these near-perfect aliases? He provided few clues in eight interviews with the HSCA. The following response to Chief Counsel Richard Sprague's questions is typical:

Sprague: What was the full name you used?

Ray: I think it was Eric S. Galt.

Sprague: Now, do you have any idea how you happened to pick that name?

Ray: I could have gotten it out of a phone book, or anything, It's something that I'd remember and it could have been, the names could have been from several different sources. I can't specifically say.

Sprague: Well, did anybody ever give you that name?

Ray: No, I don't...No one give [sic] it to me.

Asked where he got the unusual middle name "Starvo," he replied: "I couldn't say."

Ray offered only slightly more information about how he choose the Bridgeman and Sneyd aliases. He claimed that upon arriving in Toronto he searched a graveyard looking for names which he could use to apply for a passport. He continued his search by going to a

Toronto newspaper and researching old birth announcements of people "near to my own age."

It's true that birth announcements for Paul E. Bridgeman and Ramon George Sneyd appeared in two Toronto newspapers. But there are several problems with Ray's explanation. First, Sneyd and Bridgeman were born in 1932; Ray, in 1928. Why select names of men four years younger?

Second, Ray's response in no way explains how, from thousands of birth announcements, he picked two men who still lived in Toronto, near Galt and Willard, and who fit his own general physical description.

HSCA: How did...How did it come off that you happened to bear a strong physical resemblance to both Bridgeman and Sneyd?

Ray: I don't if I...I don't know if I bear a strong physical resemblance to them. Uh, uh, most these in Eng—, in Canada I don't know about now, but I don't think that'd be really something extraordinary, because most of them are the same nationality to me, English or Irish. I don't think you'd have too much problem having two features, you know. You might, I mean, there wouldn't be no radical—radical difference in appearance, Chinese or something like that.

HSCA: Well, how did you know their height and weight?

Ray: I had no idea their height and weight. I didn't know if it was similar to mine or not.

As implausible as Ray's responses were, official investigators never proposed any credible, alternative explanation. Nor did they bother to locate Willard and Bridgeman, or interview Galt. Instead, the HSCA concluded that even though the coincidences were "remarkable" and "almost" unbelievable, they were just that—coincidences. Both Ray and the committee denied the most logical possibility—that the aliases were provided to him by some person or persons involved in the crime.

The "fat man"

After Ray was arrested, his landlady on Dundas Street in Toronto, a Mrs. Loo, reported some interesting news to the police. On May 2, while Ray was hiding out in Toronto, a corpulent stranger had come to see Ramon George Sneyd (Ray's alias at the time). He'd handed Ray an envelope with a typewritten name on the front. That very day, Ray paid up his rent and spent $345 (in Canadian cash) for an airplane ticket to London.

Speculation quickly arose that this fat man was a co-conspirator or at least a courier delivering get-away money. But in less than a week, the Toronto police dramatically announced that "the fat man" had come forward, that he'd merely been returning a lost letter written by Sneyd/Ray, and that he had no involvement in the case. The man's identity was kept secret, at his request.

Was the Good Samaritan story credible, or was it more likely that Ray's escape money was in the envelope? The HSCA apparently believed the story, for they didn't bother to try to find him or investigate this angle of the case. But, again, they overlooked some suggestive details.

First, Ray's behavior that day was unusual. According to Mrs. Loo, Ray was so seldom in his room that she wasn't even sure he was occupying it, except that he did pay his rent for that week (April 26 to May 3). He was also, by all accounts, an extremely nervous fugitive. Another landlady of his in Toronto remembers him as looking "worried all the time."

A landlady in London with whom Ray stayed after leaving Toronto described him as "very, very nervous" and so reclusive that he refused to open the door to get his breakfast tray or receive telephone messages. In contrast, Ray came immediately downstairs when Mrs. Loo summoned him, as if he was expecting someone, even though he could easily have asked her to get the envelope for him.

Second, the envelope had a typewritten name on the front. Ray didn't own a typewriter nor did he have access to one, as far as we know. According to the fat man, who opened the unsealed envelope, the letter inside had something to do with a job application.

But that seems unlikely—there was only a name, no address, on the envelope. And since Ray purchased his airline ticket within hours of the incident, he either already had the money or it was delivered it to him in the envelope. Either way, job hunting made little sense for him at that time.

Third, the time frame makes it all the more likely that the fat man delivered money. On April 16, Ray had gone to the Kennedy Travel Agency in Toronto and ordered a ticket to London for May 6 and a passport under the name of Sneyd (the travel agency was handling the passport application for him).

Ray was told it would take 1–2 weeks for his application to be processed in Ottawa and mailed back to the travel agency. Ray left his Dundas Street address and Mrs. Loo's phone number with the agency.

Ten days later, on April 26, the passport arrived. It seems likely that the world's number-one fugitive would be anxious to pick up his passport and his ticket as soon as possible, in case the law began to close in—that is, unless he didn't have the money to purchase the ticket. But he didn't pick it up until May 2.

Fourth, there was a noticeable similarity between this visitor and another one during Ray's Toronto stay. His first Toronto landlady, Mrs. Szpakowski, vaguely remembered that on April 25 a visitor for Bridgeman (Ray's alias at the time) knocked on her door. He was "short, slight," had blond hair and wore a suit and tie. He held up a white envelope with the name Bridgeman typed on the front. When she informed him that "Bridgeman" had moved on and that she didn't have a forwarding address, he left.

But the strongest evidence that something more than a lost letter was involved comes from the Good Samaritan himself, whom I located in 1984. (Although he'd requested anonymity, I was able to locate him because the HSCA had failed to delete his name from one of the released documents. I'll refer to him by the pseudonym William Bolton.)

He didn't answer the front door when I knocked, but later he emerged from his back door and I was able to confront him. He appeared to be about six feet three inches tall, was powerfully built and had a large paunch.

I delivered a carefully rehearsed opening line: "I'm a professor of political science, and I'm interviewing a number of persons like yourself who had interesting encounters sixteen years ago." The logical response to such a question would, of course, be: "What are you talking about?" But Bolton was shocked.

After staring silently for a few moments, he asked, "How did you find me?" He then began to panic. "What's going on with this case?" he asked. "Is this a new investigation?" He demanded to know my identity and carefully wrote my name on a card in his wallet.

As I broached the substance of the incident, he became visibly agitated. "Nothing to it. I told them all I know." Even so, he claimed that he feared for his life. "They [the FBI] wanted me to be a witness [in 1968]. I refused. Why go [to Memphis] and get a bullet in my head?" He referred to the deaths of assassination witnesses in the John F. Kennedy case.

"Why would anyone kill you?" I asked. "Your only involvement in the case was as an innocent bystander trying to do a good deed. Substantively, there's no real involvement in the case."

He went on to explain that the people behind Ray were gangsters with big money behind them, and that the letter was about a job in Portugal that showed Ray had help. He indicated that since it was the information about Portugal that had led to Ray's arrest, he felt responsible for Ray's capture. I asked more about the letter, but he cut off the conversation with: "That's all I'll say."

Bolton's story is less than credible on two counts. First, the fat man incident didn't surface until after Ray's arrest. Since the Toronto papers gave extensive coverage to the arrest and extradition, it's highly unlikely that Bolton wouldn't have known that Ray was already behind bars before his information reached police.

Second, Bolton's account of Ray's behavior with the envelope differs from Mrs. Loo's. Bolton found Ray "nervous, scared—[he] turned his face from me and grabbed the envelope." Mrs. Loo described Ray as calm.

I was, however, impressed with one facet of his story—he seemed genuinely afraid for his personal safety, not just apprehensive about publicity. (I later learned that several weeks after my surprise visit with him, he precipitously left his job and moved away from his home.) Perhaps the most important question is who or what Bolton was afraid of. The HSCA missed a chance to find out.

If the HSCA had investigated these potentially conspiratorial aspects more thoroughly—none of which are linked to the St. Louis group—it's possible they would have reached a different conclusion about the King conspiracy. What we've discussed so far doesn't yet suggest what that conclusion might be. But if we reexamine the committee's third claim—that "no federal, state or local agency was involved in the assassination of Dr. King"—the outlines of another, more sinister, theory begin to take shape.

Chapter 4

Who was involved?

When the HSCA exonerated the government of any role in a King assassination conspiracy, their conclusion was based on a less-than-thorough review of only two government groups—the Memphis Police Department and the FBI. The evidence indicates that these groups shouldn't have been dismissed so readily, and that other government agencies may also have had a motive to kill King.

The Memphis Police Department

The Memphis Police Department (or MPD) had prepared for King's visit in three ways. First, several officers from the intelligence unit were stationed in the firehouse across from the Lorraine Motel to spy on King. Second, a four-man security detail was asssigned to protect King. Third, tactical (TACT) units for "emergency or riot situations" were created to control any violence that might erupt as a result of King's presence.

The MPD made two changes in security arrangements in the early days of April: the four-man security detail assigned to King was withdrawn 25 hours before the assassination, and three to four TACT units were pulled back from the Lorraine Motel the morning of the assassination.

The first change probably wasn't conspiratorial. King's entourage didn't want the MPD security—they perceived it as part of the hostile white power structure and so refused to divulge the details of King's itinerary. Inspector Donald Smith claimed he got tired of "tagging along" without knowing where King was headed and asked permission to withdraw the detail.

But the shift in TACT units is more disturbing. These units, each consisting of three vehicles and twelve officers, had been formed after violence erupted during King's March 28 visit to Memphis. From King's arrival on April 3 to the morning of the assassination, the units (a total of nine to twelve vehicles) were patrolling within the five to six block area "immediately surrounding" the Lorraine. On April 4, the units were pulled back to five blocks away.

The MPD's explanation—that the units withdrew because an "unidentified" member of King's entourage "instructed" them to do so—is suspect. Unlike the security detail, these units weren't there to protect King, but rather to protect the city of Memphis from the violence that might accompany King's visit.

While it's possible that King's staff would want the TACT squads kept at a distance, it's highly improbable that the MPD would comply. If anything, such a suggestion would lead police to suspect King's group was up to something. If the TACT units were in fact responding to a request that they stay out of sight, there was no need to have moved back five blocks. A distance of, say, two blocks would have been sufficient.

If the TACT vehicles had remained in place, or at least closer to the Lorraine, it would have been extremely difficult for anyone to escape the crime scene. As it was, only one unit—TACT 10—could respond quickly to news of the shooting. That's because it was taking a break in the firehouse near the Lorraine at the time King was shot.

Then there's the threat against Detective Reddit. Edward Reddit, a black Memphis police officer, was working for the MPD's intelligence squad surveilling King. According to a police memo, the MPD "received word from Washington" at 3 pm on April 4 that a "reliable informer" had advised "of a plan of the Mississippi Freedom Democratic Party, MFDP, to kill a negro Lt. here in Memphis. It is believed that they are referring to Det. Reddit." At 4:15 pm, a second MPD memo indicates that the FBI telephoned and corrected the information. It turned out that the threat was directed at a black police sergeant in Knoxville.

Either the 4:15 time of the FBI correction isn't accurate or the MPD behaved strangely after receiving the revised information. Police Chief McDonald, Inspector Tines and Public Safety Director Holloman met with Reddit between 4 and 5 pm, informing him that there was a contract out on his life, and that he and his family were to be placed under police protection.

Reddit rejected protection but was sent home anyway, accompanied by E. H. Arkin, head of the MPD's intelligence unit. The two men were sitting in front of Reddit's house in a cruiser when news of the assassination came over the police radio.

It's unclear whether Reddit's removal from the scene directly affected police performance after the assassination. The HSCA concluded that Reddit's removal from duty "was not part of any plot to facilitate the assassination of Dr. King." However, if conspirators wanted to divert the attention of key administrative and intelligence personnel during the crucial two hours before King's murder, they couldn't have done better than to inject into federal channels a false assassination plot designed to distract police from the real one.

Within a minute after King was shot, Police Officer W. B. Richmond rushed to a telephone inside the firehouse to report the shooting to intelligence headquarters. At 6:03, two minutes after the shooting, another officer (from TACT 10) radioed the police dispatcher from a patrol car parked near the firehouse.

Data continued to flow from the crime scene to police headquarters via TACT 10. At 6:07 the dispatcher was advised that a weapon had been recovered and a suspect seen running south on Main Street. At 6:08 a suspect was described as a young, well-dressed white male; there was a reference to "dark colored [inaudible]," probably dark-colored clothing. At 6:10 the getaway vehicle was described: "a late [model] white Mustang."

The MPD responded by broadcasting a "signal Q," which instructed units to maintain radio silence and await information and instructions, by ordering all downtown traffic lights switched to red to facilitate emergency traffic, and by informing the Shelby County Sheriff's Office and Tennessee Highway Patrol that King had been shot.

More important actions were taken too late or not at all. The dispatcher's order to seal off the two-block area around the Lorraine wasn't given until 6:06, three minutes after the shooting was reported. The dispatcher never issued a "signal Y," a code indicating that all main exits from Memphis should be blocked. He also never issued an APB, an all-points bulletin describing the suspect for the neighboring states of Arkansas, Mississippi and Alabama. As a result, Ray (and any others involved) slipped through each law-enforcement net that ordinarily would have trapped him.

Lt. Kallaher, the "shift commander of communications" on April 4, tried to explain these failures of communication as a result of the "massive confusion" after the assassination. But this doesn't explain why the dispatcher ordered certain procedures and not others, and the confusion wasn't reflected in the police transcripts.

The FBI

In 1968, there wasn't any good evidence that the FBI had a motive to murder King. But subsequent revelations made clear FBI director J. Edgar Hoover's hatred of King and the Bureau's attempts to destroy "the Black Messiah" personally and politically through what it called COINTELPRO ("counterintelligence program"). Yet the HSCA's investigation of the FBI employed logic so questionable it might have been lifted from a primer issued by the Warren Commission. Here are some examples.

The HSCA reasoned that if the FBI had set up the assassination, it would need to have had control over Ray. By control, the committee seems to have meant that Ray would be checked in at a motel near the Lorraine. Since Ray stayed at a distant motel his first night in Memphis and didn't move to Brewer's boarding house until the next day, the HSCA concluded that the FBI must not have had control over Ray's movements and thus didn't mastermind the assassination.

Evidently it never occurred to the committee that in a well-planned assassination, the conspirators might elect to keep their trigger man away from the target area for as long as possible to reduce the chances that he could be identified after the shooting. The committee never defended the logic that a hit man must be dispatched to the crime scene as soon as he arrives in town.

With similarly dubious reasoning, the HSCA decided that since the FBI continued its dirty tricks against King right up to the time of the assassination, the Bureau was exonerated. After all, the committee deduced,

> [i]t would hardly have been necessary to continue a nationwide program of harassment against a man soon to be killed. In a review of

all COINTELPRO files on Dr. King, the committee found substantive evidence that the harassment program showed no signs of abatement as the fateful day approached.

In other words, the HSCA didn't consider that the Bureau might be providing a cover for its complicity, or that the agents who ran COINTELPRO might not be the ones who plotted the assassination.

At the same time, the committee missed or totally neglected the fact that there was an FBI informant within the SCLC. As political scientist David J. Garrow revealed in his 1981 book *The FBI and Martin Luther King, Jr.*, "most material gathered by the FBI on King and the SCLC from mid-1966 to the time of King's death came from one human informant"—James A. Harrison. He'd joined the SCLC in 1964 and was almost immediately recruited by the Bureau, meeting weekly with his FBI handlers to provide intelligence.

On April 3, 1968, Harrison arrived in Memphis at 10:30 am. He immediately checked in with Robert Jensen, head of the FBI field office. Harrison promised he would phone in any worthwhile intelligence. He departed Memphis at 7:30 pm that same day. What, if anything, he knew about King's April 4 agenda and whether he reported anything to the Bureau remains unknown. But it does show that the HSCA missed key details in their investigation of the FBI.

The committee did, however, uncover one important piece of information—the MPD had extensive, if not unique, ties to the FBI. Public Safety Director Frank Holloman was a retired FBI agent, who'd also served as Hoover's appointments secretary and had been in charge of personnel in the director's office. Holloman described the MPD's relationship with the FBI as "very cordial and cooperative," with a flow of information that was "a two-way street."

Arkin, head of MPD intelligence, received training in Washington from at least two federal agencies (FBI and Secret Service). He boasted that he was the only police officer in the country who could walk into an FBI field office and have access to files whenever he wanted. Arkin's relationship with the FBI was so close that when he heard on his police radio that King was shot, he first called William Lawrence at the FBI field office—at 6:05 pm—not police headquarters or his intelligence units.

This close collaboration was particularly significant in the case of Marrell McCullough, a 23-year-old black undercover MPD officer. His job in the spring of 1968 was to infiltrate the Invaders, a militant black organization in Memphis that was working with King on the upcoming demonstration.

McCullough had volunteered to become "Minister of Transportation" for the Invaders as a way to gain their confidence. It was a useful role; since he transported not only the Invaders but sometimes SCLC members as well, it enabled him to keep up on what was happening in both groups.

On April 4, McCullough gave two SCLC members rides. He took an SCLC member shopping, then later picked up another member and took them both to the Lorraine, where they were to meet up with the group accompanying King to dinner. So it's possible that McCullough, among others, knew that King would emerge from his room and cross the balcony to the parking lot stairs around 6 pm for dinner.

When the HSCA investigated McCullough, they focused on the narrow question of whether he was an FBI employee. They decided he wasn't, based on the fact that when he was interviewed by the FBI after the assassination, he "was treated no differently than other eyewitnesses."

(They didn't bother to investigate whether he might have been a CIA employee, for the CIA wasn't probed at all by the HSCA. Edginton and Sergeant, however, found a confidential source in Memphis who alleged that McCullough was then working for the CIA.)

Regardless of who McCullough's employer was, the HSCA missed the crucial question. It wasn't whether McCullough was employed by federal agencies, but whether he had information that, if it ended up in federal channels, could have been tapped by conspirators in order to plan the assassination.

It's quite possible that this was the case, for McCullough's information did pass readily into federal channels. Arkin, who was McCullough's boss, kept in touch with McCullough "every other day at least." On April 2 and 3, Arkin passed data gathered by McCullough to the FBI, including information on what was happening at the Lorraine. Such knowledge would be essential for a well-orchestrated assassination plot.

The CIA

The HSCA's failure to investigate the CIA stems in part from the impression the agency sought to project—that it had only a cursory interest in King and the SCLC, and that this interest was largely satisfied by whatever data Hoover shared with the agency. The CIA describes its own King file material as routine, oriented toward matters of foreign policy and centered on world reaction to King's death. A November 28, 1975 internal memorandum even states, "we have no indication of any Agency surveillance or letter intercept which involved King."

Not many documents are publicly available to challenge this claim, but those that are tell a different story. In January 1984, in response to a Freedom of Information Act (FOIA) request, I obtained 134 pages of heavily-deleted CIA documents on "Dr. Martin Luther King, Jr." and the "Southern Christian Leadership Conference." These documents indicate that the CIA not only received FBI data on King, but that in at least two instances, it passed data to the FBI.

The documents also indicate surveillance of King; for example, there's a July 10, 1966 dispatch containing photocopies of several scrawled notes, apparently made by King or members of his staff. There are also lists of phone calls placed from his Miami hotel during a two-day period, photocopies of receipts, a page from an appointment calendar with a message for King and an assortment of business cards. There was no indication who collected the data or how it was obtained.

It's likely that much more information exists about the CIA's interest in King. In December 1990, I interviewed an ex-CIA agent who'd been a high-ranking officer and field agent. Unfortunately, I can't describe the agent, the entire interview or even why he was willing to talk to me, since these facts could reveal his identity. I also have no way to verify his allegations, but I believe his story for two reasons: the interview was arranged by a person trusted by both of us, and the source's bona fides as a CIA agent have been validated by a non-agency source I trust, by a major corporation and by a network news organization (on a story unrelated to the King case).

This ex-agent confirmed that the CIA's publicly released King file is deceptively brief. Although there were very few cables in the file, he claimed that cable traffic on King was extensive, and went back as far back as 1963. He confirmed that in the spring of 1965, CIA agents worked directly with FBI agents to bug King's Miami hotel room, but this information wasn't filed with the CIA's Office of Security (which ran domestic operations). It was filed instead with the "Western Hemisphere desk," which was responsible for the agency's vast anti-Castro operations, including the Bay of Pigs invasion.

This deceptive filing assured that the agency's politically sensitive, if not illegal, bugging of King would never pop up in domestic-surveillance files. Instead it would be cloaked by the top security of clandestine, anti-Castro operations.

Why was the CIA so interested in King? Because of its attitude toward "black power groups" and their alleged communist connections. Jay Richard Kennedy, a highly respected CIA source with close ties to the civil rights movement, warned the agency about this alleged infiltration:

> The Communist left is making an all out drive to get into the Negro movement....Communists or Negro elements who will be directed by the Communists may be in a position to, if not take over the Negro movement, completely disrupt it and cause extremely critical problems for the Government of the United States.

Kennedy believed that this wasn't simply a domestic problem, to be handled by the FBI alone, but should be considered an "international situation." So the CIA targeted black political groups with zeal. Among many activities, they infiltrated black groups participating in the Resurrection City encampment in Washington DC, photographed the participants at a Malcolm X Day rally in the Capitol, and planted an informer inside the Washington D.C. school system to report on increasing militancy among black youths.

But the main concern was what they called "Peking-line communists," whom they claimed were subverting the Vietnam War effort from within the US. Both the FBI and CIA believed that King was under communist influence—he'd not only denounced the war but allegedly had significant communist ties (an assertion the record doesn't support, by the way).

He was, moreover, a particularly dangerous figure because he'd proven his ability to mobilize a large political following. His plan for continued massive demonstrations in the spring of 1968 was apparently perceived as a major, communist-directed attempt to destabilize the US.

US intelligence was also nervous about rumors that King would launch a third-party presidential candidacy with Dr. Benjamin Spock. The FBI began gearing up "countermeasures" to deal with the candidacy, while the CIA kept their own tabs on King's plans.

For example, a CIA memo of October 5, 1967 reported that communists had tried to obtain support at the New Politics Convention for the proposed King/Spock antiwar ticket. (This three page memo is extensively censored; at least fourteen of the deletions are justified as protecting "intelligence activities, sources, or methods.")

Of course the fact that US intelligence agencies surveilled King doesn't in itself implicate those agencies in the murder; it only tells us there was interest in him and a possible motive for assassination. But some aspects of the case do point specifically to intelligence involvement.

First of all, there's Jules Ricco Kimble's alleged assassination scenario, which implicates the CIA and possibly other intelligence agencies. Ray didn't shoot King, says Kimble; he was only a patsy. The assassination was carried out by an element of US intelligence headquartered in a southern city. A "team" of seven operatives, each with specific responsibilities, was flown to a west Memphis airfield and assembled over a two-week period. Kimble himself flew in the two "snipers" who were to do the shooting with rifles identical to Ray's.

One of the team's "intelligence types" obtained three Memphis Police uniforms to be worn by operatives at the crime scene. Two of these operatives were snipers who concealed themselves in the bushes behind the boarding house (the second sniper acting as a backup shot if needed).

After one fired the shot, both concealed their rifles in a prearranged hiding place behind the boarding house (where they'd later be retrieved by other operatives). The two snipers then jumped down onto the sidewalk from the bushes and mingled with the other uniformed officers who were rushing about.

Kimble says that a method of verifying the credentials of the police impostors had been established. Should any of the real police notice the unknown officers, they would be told to phone a particular MPD captain who would vouch for the "new" men. The team also had an unmarked van with sophisticated electronic radio equipment; it could oversee the crime scene as well as monitor and broadcast on police radio channels. Kimble also says that someone else dropped the bundle.

How credible is Kimble? He claims that he's talking now because his former sponsors have double-crossed him in a prison drug bust to keep him in jail. He wants to tell some secrets in retaliation. But Sergeant and Edginton warn that "one must begin with the assumption that everything Kimble says is rubbish and go on from there [to prove or disprove him]."

I, too, think that some of Kimble's specific allegations are false—some most likely reflect ignorance or misinformation he's received, and others may be outright fabrications. But remember that he didn't bring his story to any researchers or journalists; he only began to admit involvement and discuss the conspiracy in the course of the interview with the British journalists, after I had gathered data documenting his possible involvement. Since some aspects of his story have been found credible (there was, for example, a CIA identities specialist in Montreal as Kimble claimed), it's certainly worth investigating his story.

Another aspect of the case that points to involvement by the intelligence community is the physical similarity between Ray and the four men whose names he used as aliases (as described above). This reflects a sophisticated access to data that was surely beyond either the capacities of a small-time loser like Ray or the alleged St. Louis plotters with their primitive assassination scenario, especially since all these aliases were the names of men who lived in Toronto, a city Ray had never visited until after the assassination.

The Galt alias is particularly suspect. I've corresponded with and interviewed Eric Galt, to try to determine why Ray chose his name as his chief alias. Here are my speculations about what might have happened.

In 1968 Galt worked for Union Carbide of Canada Ltd. (as he had since the early 1950s), in an area of the plant that had a very special assignment—ongoing research and development for a defense device called "the proximity fuse." This work was highly secret, and all employees on the project at Carbide's Toronto plant underwent intensive and periodic security checks conducted by the RCMP (Royal Canadian Mounted Police). Galt's last security clearance check was in 1961, seven years before the assassination. He describes his RCMP file as extensive, containing background information as well as his physical characteristics.

Ray's use of the Galt alias at times reflects the data in Galt's file, suggesting that Ray somehow had access to that information. For example, when Ray was in Montreal in 1967 seeking to establish credentials in Galt's name, he wrote the Canadian Department of Veterans Affairs posing as Galt.

Galt wasn't a veteran, but it would be known from his RCMP security file that he'd applied to the Canadian Air Force for enlistment early in WWII, that he'd been asked by Carbide not to enlist because he was needed for defense work and that Carbide then arranged for a civilian deferment. We don't know the contents of the letter, but Ray was probably hoping, at the very least, to get a response from the department and thus generate more "Galt paper."

Ray also allegedly wrote a letter to the South African Counsel concerning the possibility of immigrating to Rhodesia. From the file Ray would have known that Galt's father had once been a prominent private detective in South Africa and had emigrated to Canada before Galt was born. Again, the letter was probably intended to generate a paper trail in Galt's name. It may also have been written to prepare for Ray's get-away after the assassination, since his final destination was Africa.

If that's the case, the letter shows premeditation on Ray's part. (Or it's possible that someone other than Ray wrote the letter, arranging for Ray's role as hit man or assassin. None of the four fingerprints on the letter are Ray's; further identification of them hasn't been made.)

There's also the change in Galt's signature—from Eric St. Vincent (which, when signed, looked like Starvo) to Eric S. Galt. At the time of Galt's last security check in 1961, he was still using the longer signature. When he shortened it in 1966, he did so in part because Carbide's computer system preferred the simplicity of using only a middle initial. The change was also in his file. Perhaps Ray's switch from Starvo to S. was done so that Ray's cover would seem all the more like the real Galt.

If Ray did have access to the information in Galt's file, we know that it had to have been provided to him by someone else. There are several ways this could have been done— each involves US intelligence agencies.

First, US intelligence might have had a behind-the-scenes security role at Union Carbide of Canada, which was 75% American-owned. Galt and his coworkers had the impression that the proximity fuse was basically an American invention (an impression later confirmed by my interview with a retired US Air Force colonel, who'd been involved in weapons research and development in the late 1960s). So it's conceivable that US intelligence was present at Carbide in order to insure that US military secrets were safe there.

Second, dossiers might have been traded or requested from the RCMP (ostensibly for a purpose unrelated to the assassination) by the CIA or some other US intelligence agency. In the 1960s, the RCMP and the CIA worked closely together, attempting to destroy KGB spy networks in North America.

Third, Galt's file might have been obtained through some quasi-official, highly secretive intelligence network in which a group of public agencies had private agreements to share data. One example of such an organization was the Law Enforcement Intelligence Unit (LEIU), a private association of police intelligence squads formed in 1956. This organization served as a clearinghouse for intelligence data; it exchanged at will dossiers on known criminals, private citizens and political figures—without regard for right-of-privacy restraints.

According to former CIA computer expert and Branch Chief George O'Toole, LEIU linked "intelligence squads of almost every major police force in the United States and Canada." LEIU, or some similar entity, could have been the source for matching Ray (through his prison file) with Galt (through his security file).

The secondary aliases could have been obtained from the same source that provided the Galt information or from other files. Peter Dale Scott, a former Canadian diplomat with expertise in intelligence agencies, has said that it's fairly easy to select three or four names with similar physical characteristics if one has access to government files.

The names could have come from such sources as the passport office, Toronto police files (Sneyd was a Toronto police officer) and files on municipal employees (Bridgeman worked for the Toronto Board of Education). Or the names could have been selected from a more generic data bank, like driver's license applications.

How were the aliases to be used? The plan seems to have been to implicate the real Eric Galt in the crime, giving Ray time to get out of the country (although it's still not clear why Ray took so long to leave Canada).

That plan was partially successful. Authorities quickly established a trail pointing to the innocent Eric Galt—his name was on the motel register where Ray stayed in Memphis April 3, and the abandoned car thought to be the get-away vehicle was registered in his name. Ray's secondary aliases also helped implicate Galt.

Since it made sense to authorities that a man plotting an assassination would use aliases for activities directly connected to the crime, they deduced that the suspect's real name was Galt, and that he'd used an alias to buy the rife and another to rent a room near King. Since the latter alias (John Willard) lived near Galt in Toronto, it would seem possible that Galt had somehow usurped Willard's name after spotting him there. Galt could have noted the resemblance between them and found a way to learn Willard's name.

If authorities had located Galt before the search turned to Ray, Galt would have been a likely assassin. He was an expert marksman and frequently traveled with guns in his car. A check into his family background would have revealed his father's detective work in South Africa, one of the world's most racist societies (thus possibly establishing a motive). And authorities would have found that Galt frequently made trips to the southern US; he'd visited Birmingham, where the rifle was purchased, and Memphis, the scene of the crime.

Fortunately for the real Galt, authorities weren't able to locate him until April 18. On that day the Kansas City field office of the FBI cabled J. Edgar Hoover and the Memphis field office that they'd located an Eric Galt in the Toronto telephone directory. The FBI immediately began investigating, but the search was called off when, within hours, Ray's prints were identified on the rifle.

My account of how and why Ray came to use Galt's name, although speculative, does point to US intelligence as the most likely source of Ray's aliases. When combined with the other questions about government involvement, these speculations suggest, at the very least, that the HSCA's blanket exoneration of federal, state and local agencies was unwarranted. Those agencies haven't been investigated fully enough to absolve them of a role in the crime.

Chapter 5

Solving the case

In 1978, the HSCA turned its findings over to the Justice Department and suggested further investigation. A decade later, the Justice Department claimed that all known leads had been checked and that "[n]o further investigation appears to be warranted...unless new information...becomes available."

Further investigation is warranted, for several reasons. First, the HSCA inquiry was glaringly inadequate. It's shameful that an investigation into the death of a man as important to this country's past and future as Martin Luther King, Jr., a man whom we now honor with a national holiday, was conducted so shabbily. He and his family—as well as the nation—deserve the full truth.

Second, the case has new leads, people and topics to be probed. If they're pursued, the question "who killed Martin Luther King?" may now be answerable. The following is not an exhaustive list, but a selection of some of the most important leads:

- All witness and law-enforcement personnel should be interviewed about what they might have seen in the bushes behind the boarding house. The results of the footprint analysis in the yard should be obtained.

- Neutron activation tests and ballistics-comparison tests should be conducted by independent experts.

- Unidentified fingerprints on items in the bundle and in the boarding house should be compared with the prints of all persons, including Kimble, who are targets for investigation.

- "Ted Andrews" should be questioned about the conflicts and gaps in his story. His military records and all FBI files pertaining to him should be examined.

- Jules Ricco Kimble's possible relationship to the CIA should be examined. The agency should be required to provide its Kimble file as well as other data that might shed light on his alleged CIA involvement.

- The US telephone numbers of Kimble's calls from his Montreal girlfriend's apartment should be investigated.

- All available pictures of Memphis Police at the crime scene should be analyzed in light of Kimble's allegations. All those in uniform should be identified; the presence of an unmarked van should be checked.

- "William Bolton" must be located, protected, questioned and subjected to a complete background check.

- All Memphis Police officers who might have knowledge of the withdrawal of the tactical units should be questioned under oath.

- All persons involved in the false death threat against Detective Reddit should be questioned under oath.

- Marrell McCullough's possible relationship to the CIA should be probed.

- Reputed CIA identities expert Raoul Miora should be questioned. CIA officers who served in Canada during the relevant period should be interviewed, as should Union Carbide security officials.

- The National Security Agency, Defense Department, Air Force and CIA should be formally queried about any information they might have concerning Ray's aliases.

- The FBI and CIA should be required to produce all documents concerning their attempt to influence history or public opinion about the King case.

- The HSCA's files should be released to the public. Despite the committee's failures, their key documents and interviews could help to pursue the above leads. The film *JFK* evoked public pressure to release the HSCA's Kennedy files, but Congress still intends to keep its King files secret until the year 2028.

Who should conduct the investigation? It shouldn't be the FBI—even after two decades, the Bureau has at least a historical conflict of interest. Nor should the Justice Department have a primary role, due to its secrecy and inactivity during the decade following the HSCA's investigation. And another congressional effort would very likely become mired in the web of politics and personalities spawned by the previous committee.

The best alternative—although not without pitfalls—is to appoint a special prosecutor.

The appointment should be made after consulting with prominent black leaders and, certainly, with the King family. This should be done soon, before the tide of intrigue and disinformation, as well as the passage of time, obscure this chance for the US justice system to live up to its professed ideals.

Recommended reading

Garrow, David. *The FBI and Martin Luther King, Jr.* Penguin Books, 1983.

Halpern, Morton et al. *The Lawless State : The Crimes of U.S. Intelligence Agencies.* Penguin Books, 1976.

Select Committee on Assassinations, U.S. House of Representatives. *The Final Assassinations Report.* Bantam, 1979.

Weisberg, Harold. *Frame-up.* Outerbridge and Dienstfrey, 1971.

Notes

Sources for the facts in this book are listed below by page numbers and brief subject descriptions. Full publication data is given the first time a work is cited (except for the four books listed on the previous page; to remind you where to look, their names are bolded the first time they're cited below).

Chapter 1

5. SCLC denounces war. *Newsweek,* April 10, 1967, 32.

5. Riverside church speech. *Freedomways,* Spring 1967, 105, 109, 113–14.

5–6. Massive civil disobedience. *US News and World Report*, August 28, 1967, 10.

6. Criticism of King. *Life*, April 21, 1967, 4.

6. LBJ's fear. Mark Lane and Dick Gregory. *Code Name "Zorro"* Prentice-Hall, 1977, 52.

7–8. King's murder. **HSCA *Report,*** 368–69.

8–9. US response to King's death. Lewis Chester, Godfrey Hodgson, and Bruce Page, *An American Melodrama: The Presidential Campaign of 1968,* Viking, 1969, 16–17.

9. Clark's optimism. "U.S. Attorney General Confident King's Murderer Will Be Found," *Memphis Press Scimitar,* April 5, 1968, 13.

9–10. Ray's guilty plea. James Earl Ray. *Who Killed Martin Luther King?,* National Press Books, 1992, 115–134.

11–13. Evidence against Ray. HSCA *Report,* 376, 380–81, 386–87; Bessie Brewer, FBI interview April 13, 1968 (44–1987 Sub D–74), 7 pp. at pp. 1–2.

13. Dollahite's report. Vernon Dollahite, FBI interview April 13, 1968 (44–1987 Sub D–75).

13. Bundle contents. HSCA *Report*, 29.

14–16. Ray's defense. Ray, 61–111.

16. No government involvement. HSCA *Report,* 533.

Chapter 2

17. Sniper's location. HSCA *Report,* 375.

18. HSCA relies on earwitnesses. HSCA *Report,* 378.

18–20. Renting the room. Bessie Brewer, FBI interview April 13, 1968 (44–1987 Sub D–74) 7 pp. at p. 2; HSCA *Report,* 380–87.

21–22. Stephens' testimony. FBI statements of April 7 and 10, 1968; FBI interviews: April 10, 1968 (44–1987– Sub D78), 5 pp; April 7, 1968 (44–1987–Sub D–16), 2 pp.

22. Anshutz' testimony. FBI interview April 7, 1968 (14–1987–Sub D4) 1 p.

23. Stephens' drinking. US Congress, House. *Hearings on the Investigation of the Assassination of Martin Luther King, Jr.* (HSCA), vols. 1–13. US Govt. Printing Office, 1979, vol. 13, 285–87.

23. Stephens' affidavit. **Harold Weisberg**, appendix.

23–24. Stephens changes story. Tom Jones, "Man Claims He's Entitled to Rewards in King Slaying," *Memphis Press Scimitar,* Jan. 21, 1974, 15; James Cole, "Witness Says He Hoped to Collect King Reward," *Memphis Commercial Appeal,* Jan. 22, 1974, 15.

24. Grace Stephens' testimony. FBI interview April 6, 1968 (14–1987– Sub D4) 1 p.; HSCA *Report*, 402–4.

24–25. Solomon Jones interview. FBI, April 13, 1968 (ME44–1987 Sub D–76), 4 pp., at p. 3.

25. HSCA discounts G. Stephens, Carter and Jones. HSCA *Report,* 373, 408; *HSCA,* vol.13, 4; Bessie Brewer: FBI interview, April 13, 1968 (44–1987–Sub–D–74), 7 pp.

25. Footprints near cellar door. Landers, FBI interview, May 15, 1968 (ME–1987 Sub–D–77), 2 pp.

25. Plaster cast results unknown. Howard Teten: FBI interview, April 4, 1968 (44–1987 Sub D) [unintelligible], 2 pp. at p. 1.

26–27. Ray's fingerprints. *HSCA,* vol. 13, 113; HSCA *Report,* 381.

27. Missing fingerprints. Weisberg, 209.

28. Other prints in Ray's room. *HSCA,* vol. 13, 112.

28–30. Ballistics evidence. HSCA *Report* , 382–83; *HSCA,* vol. 13, 56, 63–64, 66–67.

30–31. What bullet comparisons might show. Kurtz, *Crime of the Century,* University of Tennessee Press, 104–6.

31-32. Polygraph evidence. *HSCA,* vol. 13, 145–51.

Chapter 3

33–35. St. Louis conspiracy. HSCA *Report* , 470–90, 644.

35. Dodd's dissent. HSCA *Report,* 644.

36. Canipe's witnesses. Graham FBI interview, 2, 380–1.

36. Press reports on white Mustangs. Weisberg, 181, 183.

36–37. Mustang sightings. HSCA *Report,* 387; Jowers, FBI interview April 7, 1968 (ME 44–1987 Sub D–92), 2 pp. at p. 1; Cupples, FBI interview April 15, 1968 (ME 44–1987 Sub D–93), 2 pp. at p. 1; Reed, FBI interview May 15, 1968 (ME 44–1987 Sub D–102), 2 pp. Hendrix, FBI interview April 25, 1968 (Sub D–103), 2 pp.; Parker, FBI interview April 15, 1968 (ME 44–1968 Sub D–54) , 2 pp.;

Copeland, FBI interview April 17, 1968 (ME 44–1987 Sub
D–14), 1 p.; Thompson, FBI interview April 17, 1968 (ME
44–1987–Sub D–15), 1 p.; Weisberg, 182–84; "'Sing It
Real Pretty' Was Last Request of Civil Rights Leader,"
Memphis Commercial Appeal, April 6, 1968, 1.

37. York Arms clerk's estimate. Carpenter, FBI interview
April 15, 1968 (ME 44–1987 Sub D–64), 3 pp. at p. 1.

38. Jowers' testimony. Jowers, FBI interview April 7, 1968
(ME 44–1987 Sub D–92), 2 pp. at p. 1–2.

39. FBI clears Andrews. FBI memo June 24, 1968
(44–1987 Sub–234), 1 p.

40. Deletions in Andrews' file. FBI document (44–1987
Sub B–69C), memo from Agent Franklin L. Johnson, April
10, 1968, Special Agent in Charge (SAC) Memphis, 2 pp.
at p. 1.

41. Ray's Raoul story, HSCA *Report,* 394–6.

41. *HSCA* 467. HSCA's tries to implicate Ray's brothers.
HSCA *Report,* 456–70.

41–42. Salwyn's findings. Author's interview with Salwyn,
Toronto, Sept. 12,1984; two follow-up telephone interviews, Sept. 16 and 17, 1984. Salwyn's account was cor-
roborated by Earl McRae (interviewed in Toronto, Sept.
12, 1984).

42. HSCA's analysis of Kimble's role. HSCA *Report,* 514–15.

42–43. Oster's investigation. Author's telephone interviews with Joseph Oster, October 5, 8; November 13, 18,
1985.

44–45. Ray's aliases. *HSCA,* vol. 3, 46–47, 136, 143,
246–51, 174–75; vol. 9, 283–89, 291, 332–34, 343–45,
421, 425, 475; vol. 10, 80, 373; vol. 11, 23–28, 413–
14, 417–27; telephone conversation with Harold
Weisberg, Sept. 5, 1984.

45. Sinister implications of aliases. *HSCA,* vol. 5, 10.

46. Physical characteristics of Ray's aliases. Jay Walz, "3 Whose Names Ray Used Resemble Him," *New York Times,* June 12, 1968, 1; Cameron Smith and Loren Lind, "How Did Ray Get Names of 3 Whose Description Fit His?" *Toronto Globe and Mail,* June 11, 1968, 5; *HSCA,* vol. 11, 39–40 (on Sneyd and Bridgeman).

48–49. Ray accounts for aliases to HSCA. *HSCA,* vol. 9, 281–84.

49. Birth announcements. *HSCA,* vol. 11, 24–25, 39–40.

50. Aliases coincidental. *HSCA,* vol. 5, 11–12.

51–52. The "fat man." "Who's the Fat Man?", *Toronto Star,* June 10, 1968, 1; Homer Bigart "Mounties Hunt 'Fat Man' in Ray Case," *New York Times,* June 10,1968, 1; "Suspect: Police After Two Men Seen with Him," *Toronto Telegram,* June 10, 1968, 11; Cameron Smith and Loren Lind, "Fat Man Visits Ray, Landlady Recalls," *Toronto Globe and Mail,* June 10, 1968, 1; "Cabby: I Picked up 'Fat Man' in King Killer Case, *Toronto Star,* June 12, 1968, 1; "'Fat Man' Cleared in King Killer Case," *Toronto Star,* June 13, 1968, 2; "'Fat Man' Cleared in Ray Case Probe," Ward Just, *Washington Post ,* June 14, 1968, A–5; author's interview with McRae, Sept. 12, 1984; telephone conversations with Mrs. Yee Sun Loo and son, Sept. 25, 1984.

52. Envelope for Bridgeman. Jay Walz, "3 Men Whose Names Ray Used,"*New York Times,* June 12, 1968, 1; "Fat Man Cleared in King Killer Case," *Toronto Star,* June 13, 1968, 2; "Cabbie: I Picked up 'Fat Man' in King Killer Case," *Toronto Star,* June 12, 1968, 1.

53. William Bolton. Author's interview with Bolton, 1984, Canada.

55. No government involvement. HSCA *Report ,* 533.

Chapter 4

56–57. King's group's response to MPD. Author's interview with Rev. Samuel Kyles, Memphis, Jan. 10, 1986.

57. TACT units formed. HSCA *Report* , 558; *HSCA,* vol. 4, 278, 282.

57. TACT units pulled back. Affidavit of Officer William O. Crumby, *HSCA,* vol. 4, 279–80.

57. Purpose of TACT units. Interview with Rev. Samuel Kyles, Memphis, Jan. 10, 1986; Holloman testimony, *HSCA,* vol. 4, 278.

58–59. Detective Reddit. HSCA *Report,* 550–59; *HSCA,* vol. 4, 267, 269; MPD memo, "Tines to McDonald"; MPD memo from Arkin to Tines "Threat on Negro Lt. Memphis Police Department," April 4, 1968; author's interview with E. H. Arkin, Memphis, Jan. 10, 1986.

59–60. Data from crime scene. HSCA *Report,* 559–60; transcript of TACT 10 and dispatcher, *HSCA,* vol. 4, 290–317; 287–89.

60. Lt. Kallaher's explanation. *HSCA,* vol. 4, 287, affidavit of MPD Lt. Frank Kallaher.

61–62. HSCA absolves FBI. HSCA *Report,* 538, 542.

62. Informant James Harrison. **David J. Garrow,** 11, 175, 198.

63. MPD's ties to FBI. *HSCA,* vol. 4, 233, 236, 243, 325.

63–65. Marrell McCullough. *HSCA,* vol. 6, 428, 440–1, 443; FBI memo William H. Lawrence to Sac, "Cominfil of SNCC," April 3, 1968, in FBI file "Memphis Sanitation Workers' Strike" (157–1092–232) 1–2, 4; see also FBI file "Invaders," (157–8490).

65. CIA's interest in King. See internal memorandum, November 28, 1975, subject: "Martin Luther King, Jr."; compare with Oct. 5, 1967 memo concerning King's activities in Chicago which CIA passed on to the FBI. Forty of the 134 pages released to the author involve domestic surveillance of King prior to his death, and an active interest in King's domestic political activities.

67. Kennedy quote. "Memorandum for the Record," May 11, 1965, CIA Office of Security.

67. An "international situation." Garrow, 141

67–68. CIA infiltration. "CIA Infiltrated Black Groups Here in the 1960s," *Washington Post,* March 30, 1978, A1.

68. King's alleged communist ties. "Memorandum for the Record," May 11, 1965, CIA Office of Security; Garrow, 143–44; CIA "Memorandum for Chief, Security Research Staff, subject deleted, Feb. 8, 1968.

70. Kimble's credibility. David Mendelsohn's interview of Sargeant. January 15, 1990, WBAI radio, New York.

71–72. Speculations on the Galt alias. Telephone interview with Eric Galt, March 26 and June 27, 1984.

73. Proximity fuse an American invention. David C. Martin, *Wilderness of Mirrors ,* Ballantine Books, 1983, 165–66.

74. LEIU links with police. George O'Toole, *The Private Sector,* W. W. Norton, 1978, 146.

Chapter 5

77. Justice Dept. denies investigation is needed. *Boston Herald,* September 4, 1988, 2.

Index

More books in the Real Story series
(see the next page for other titles)

The Decline and Fall of the American Empire
Gore Vidal

Vidal is one of our most important—and wittiest—social critics. This little book is the perfect introduction to his political views.

Burma: The Next Killing Fields?
Alan Clements

If we don't do something about Burma, it will become another Cambodia. Written by one of the few Westerners ever to have lived there, this book tells the story vividly.

Who Killed JFK?   Carl Oglesby

This brief but fact-filled book gives you the inside story on the most famous crime of this century. You won't be able to put it down.

Real Story books are available at most good bookstores, or send $5 per book + $2 shipping *per order* (not per book) to Odonian Press, Box 7776, Berkeley CA 94707. Please write for information on quantity discounts, or call us at 800 REAL STORY or 510 524 4000.

The Real Story series
is based on a simple idea—
political books don't have to be boring.
Short, well-written and to the point,
Real Story books are meant to be <u>read</u>.

If you liked this book,
check out some of the others:

Who Killed Robert Kennedy?

Philip Melanson

This provocative book explores numerous loop-holes in the official explanation of the RFK assassination, and points to possible culprits.

Spring, 1993

The Greenpeace Guide to Anti-environmental Organizations   Carl Deal

This comprehensive guide describes dozens of industry front groups that masquerade as environmental organizations.   *Spring, 1993*

What Uncle Sam Really Wants

Noam Chomsky

A brilliant analysis of the real motivations behind US foreign policy, from one of America's most popular speakers. Full of astounding information.

For information on other books (and how to order),
see the previous page.